Now What?

A New Perspective and How to Live It

Dusty Farrell

ISBN: 0-9833776-4-2

ISBN-13: 978-0-9833776-4-1

DEDICATION

To those who kept me on tract without realizing how I saw the Lord in them at a time I thought He was not in me, to my family. To our future generations, I saw you from afar, these words describe your heritage.

CONTENTS

ACKNOWLEDGMENTS

My friend, Roy Blizzard, III, who is a constant encouragement and inspiration.

My old buddy, Mike Gaskin, who is a missionary in Mexico and is a trusted friend and the great photographer of the picture on the cover. This sun is rising over the hills near his home in Leon, Mexico.

My nephew, Davey, who designed the cover.

PREFACE

I'm sure you have become excited about what's happening in your life with the Lord. I expect a whole new world has appeared and bringing such promise you can't sleep. I know how things can begin to make a little sense, maybe for the first time.

I want to remind you of Paul's letter to the Colossians, 1:4-23. Just as he told them, receive these words afresh personally. All I can say is, Wow!

Paul noted how people were affected by the message which shows them the Truth of the Good News because they could grasp love on a deeper spirit level and the associated hope laid up for them in heaven. Don't put heaven off for a time after the body dies. Yes, we will have more afterward than now, but we can also have His type of life here, in this time.

You may have noticed I don't use the word "spiritual" very much. This word has a different meaning for each person who uses it, thus would cloud what I want to say. But times do come along when its use is compelling.

Then Paul began to tell them how he prayed for them, we can pray the same now as well so let's make this personal. We pray how we are to be filled with the complete understanding of His will in ALL spiritual wisdom together with a growing awareness of the spirit realm. Further, we should walk, or conduct ourselves in a manner worthy of the Lord and His grace we are experiencing. Furthermore, we should be stimulated and energized as spirit by the capacity for valor delivered to us by His glory combined with Joy! We should give thanks to the Father Who has made us fit and able to share the inheritance of the saints in the Light. He delivered us out of darkness and translated us into the kingdom of His Son, Who is the product of His absolute Love.

Verse 19, it pleased the Father for ALL the divine fullness should dwell in Jesus as a bodily form, forever. This perfectly defines the term "glory."

1
NEW LIFE

There may be some folks who, as a result of the work of the Holy Spirit, need the following information. If so, this is how you begin.

Romans 10:9-13,
… if you shall confess with your mouth Jesus (as) Lord, and shall believe in your heart that God raised Him from the dead, you shall be saved: 10) for with the heart, (the eternal spirit/soul combination), man believes unto righteousness (a prepared place of standing to be occupied); and with the mouth confession is made unto salvation (a saving wholeness). 11) For the scripture says, whosoever believes on Him shall not be put to shame. 12) For there is no distinction (as spirit man) between Jew and Greek: for

the same (Lord) is Lord of all, and is rich unto all that call upon Him: 13) for, whosoever shall call upon the name of the Lord shall be saved (made alive in spirit). ASV

You're possibly reading this book because something happened to you as you read my book, **"Who Is the End Time Church? Recognizing the Spirit Realm."** The Lord has opened your eyes and you're seeing yourself in a new light and you have a new reference point. You truly see yourself as a spirit man, male or female and it is the real man, not the false reality man. You also see your Father in new light so you know I have no words to describe Him, none are needed. The Bible will now be clearer as you read it as well.

If you've never personally known the Lord in this manner, there is something to be done as shown in Romans 10. You have the wonderful opportunity, with your spirit eyes open, with your whole heart, to now confirm your belief about Jesus concerning what He has accomplished for the real man you are, male or female; by doing so you will receive absolute life and enter into a perfect union with Him. It is a new, wonderful condition of your life which explains why He is The Savior and there's no other.

This spirit union of God and man is one of a renewed blood covenant which Jesus initiated on man's behalf and has committed to perform on your behalf, so much so, when He joins Himself to you no discernable difference can remain. Jesus said He will never leave us nor forsake us, you're now included.

Having believed the report about Him, Paul wrote detailing how confession is made unto salvation, a term better understood as wholeness. Right now, tell the Lord how you feel and all the thoughts you're having toward Him. Commit yourself completely to Him. Don't ever again dwell on any self demeaning thoughts about yourself nor believe He is separated from you. Instead, focus on yourself as spirit and trust Him to cleanse you of all unrighteousness, meaning when you act inconsistently as this new person, tell Him and forget it.

Don't do or say anything which doesn't flow from the influence of the new, recreated man including church attendance, giving, scripture study, prayer, etc. Jesus said the true worshippers of the Father must do so in Spirit and in Truth. You are now enabled by the Holy Spirit to do this exactly, any time and any place.

You must give Him something to work with in your life and the requirement is what Paul instructed to Timothy, bring every thought captive to the obedience of Christ. Your thoughts are the only thing you have the power to control and the new spirit man must now begin to directly influence your thought life (this is obedience) as compared to the standard of what we see in Jesus as recorded in the Gospels. Don't allow anything to dwell in your mind contrary to yourself as His perfect child, you are just like Him in essence, He will now teach you how to exist and how to live in His system of government.

Always keep this in mind; the words of man can do nothing without the Holy Ghost. He is our Teacher and Guide in the new life and He alone gets the credit.

There's one more step which carries tremendous symbolism with great power due to your new perspective, water baptism. The church has much controversy concerning the subject and it is all a distraction as you are about to see.

Here are several verses about baptism and its meaning and you'll clearly see why it's important.

Colossians 2:11-14,
… in Whom (Jesus) you were also circumcised with a circumcision not made with hands, in the putting (stripping) off of the body of the (His)

flesh, in the circumcision of Christ (His Spirit example); 12) having been buried with Him in (your) baptism (immersion in water), wherein you were also raised with Him through faith in the working of God, who raised Him (and now you) from the dead. 13) And you, being dead through your trespasses and the uncircumcision of your flesh (as mentioned above), you, (I say), did He make alive together with Him, having forgiven us all our trespasses; 14) having blotted out the bond written in ordinances (the old moral and ceremonial law) that was against us, which was contrary to us: and He had taken it out of the way, nailing it to the cross (you then live from and walk in learning the ways of the spirit realm as a resident of the kingdom of God); ASV

1 Peter 3:20-4:2,
(Noah and his family) were saved through water: 21) which also after a true likeness (or picture to show how it) does now save you, (even true) baptism, not the putting away of the filth of the flesh, but the examination (or an appeal from an intense desire) of a good (clear) conscience toward God, through the resurrection of Jesus Christ (because the spirit is made alive); 22) Who is on the right hand of God, having gone into heaven; angels and authorities and powers being made subject unto Him.

4:1) Forasmuch then as Christ suffered (as a spirit man) in the flesh, arm yourselves also with the same (renewed) mind; for he that has suffered in the flesh (in the same way) has ceased from sin; 2) that you no longer should live the <u>rest of your time in flesh</u> (subject) to the lusts of men, but to the will of God. ASV

Romans 6:3-7,
Or are you ignorant that all we who were baptized (immersed) into Christ Jesus were baptized (immersed) into His death? 4) We were buried therefore with Him through baptism unto death: that like as Christ was raised from the dead through the glory (fullness of attributes) of the Father, so we also might <u>walk in newness of life</u>. 5) For if we have become united with (Him) in the likeness of his death, we shall be also (in the likeness) of His resurrection (life); 6) knowing this, that our old man was crucified with (Him), that the body of sin might be done away, that so we should no longer be in bondage to (the body of) sin; 7) for he that has died is justified (through Christ) (and released) from sin. ASV

Notice how resurrection is mentioned with each passage, this is the power of water baptism and the new born spirit man which you are. You have experienced the literal resurrection power flowing outward from the very resurrection of the Lord Jesus as Paul described in Philippians 3.

Water baptism declares for all, including you, how you are raised a new creature, recreated in Christ, exactly like Him as our example.

The real eternal you has been raised to a new existence, similar to Jesus and later, at the end of this era, exactly like Him.

Don't get caught up in the useless arguments over how this is done, this a statement you make in agreement with the Lord's statement about you, demonstrating your new condition of existence by following the same path, symbolically, with the same knowledge, literally, as Jesus.

I must say it again; you are following the same path with the same knowledge as Jesus which culminated in the resurrection and total fulfillment of His person including a spirit body.

Through water baptism you now fully identify with Him! Your attitude is the key. You now know what the reason is and what your claim is to being related to Him.

Here is what has happened, you have repented. No one is excluded and there are no time limits.

Acts 2:38-39,
And Peter (said) unto them, Repent, and be baptized every one of you in the name of Jesus Chr-

ist unto the remission of your sins; and you shall receive the gift of the Holy Spirit. 39 For to you is the promise, and to your children, and to all that are afar off, (even) as many as the Lord our God shall call unto Him.

Repentance describes the 180 degree turning; you were living and moving in one direction, the soul/body oriented, material world as we know it, to now going a completely opposite direction toward the spirit reality as designed, spirit/soul/body. You have turned from a carnal life to a spirit life, a carnal existence to a spirit existence. The essence of "being" has changed and you are made new by the power of God.

Paul explained it like this, if you have died with Christ to material ways of looking at things and have escaped from the personal effect on you of the world's crude and elemental notions and teachings of externalism, why would you still live as if you belong to the world? The answer is we are now able to live focused on Jesus and His life we now have together as spirit, Paul went on to say in Colossians.

2
SONSHIP

The new life for us is one of sonship.

Ladies keep in mind this spirit context for you functions just as would a son in his father's house, a position of authority, privilege and equality as on the sixth day of creation. To God there is no difference.

One friend, who read my book through only one time, said nothing registered with him. Since he knew me, he decided maybe he was distracted or in a hurry so he started reading again. Once he was about half-way he said something seemed to explode from within him. Clarity hit his mind and everything, absolutely everything changed. It was then he realized himself as spirit man made in the image and likeness of his Father, he realized his sonship of the Creator. He saw his world and family in different light as well.

He called me to report what happened and like others who have done the same I recognized in his words the life and truth of the kingdom of God. This is unmistakable. We decided to meet and talk about his eye opening experience; we set a time for a few days later.

Some people have no reaction at all and some seem to only get a glimpse of the spirit man as my friend first mentioned when he read the book through only once. I wondered what the result over the next few days would be, a complete loss of the effect or the start of a personal settling I know so well. I expected his words to reveal this without a description on his part.

When we met, together with our wives, my wife and I could tell he was a changed man, truly and deeply at peace for the first time since I had met him about ten years earlier. He began to explain to us about what happened to his mind, from the first event and then throughout the days leading up to our meeting. He marveled at his unshakable peace and how he could now see and understand scriptures which for years had been out of reach to his understanding. He was amazed how his point of view for life had shifted to himself as a spirit son of Elohiym the Creators. This son was made perfect by the Blood of Jesus and he realized his self doubt and sin could not touch the reborn man of the heart to disqualify him from blessing. He also saw the end result is wholeness, meaning the reunion of the man as Holy Spirit unified or infused with man's spirit and soul which abides in the body.

He wondered how he could have missed this all the years he had been a Christian and attended church. How could men be blind yet talk about the Lord and man as a spirit being?

Because my friend is a man conditioned to read and study about the Lord, he expected the same process needed to continue, so already in this new context his mind was searching for things he needed to do. His question of the evening to me was:

Now what?

I started writing about this life as a blog for my kids who are grown and moved away. They wanted a reference available for themselves at anytime, something to go by when teaching their children. It was then titled "Foundations." Honestly, I gave little thought about what people, having a similar experience, would do who I don't know. Now my mind was searching to find things for me to do about this type of question. I did tell him I planned to write another book, not this one, and he thought I should hurry with the work. I have worked on it a bit since then.

Up till now, as I write, we've met three more times over lunch, without the ladies. The first time we didn't talk about what happened, I usually allow conversations to flow where they will. I only speak when the opportunity opens to me.

The next two meetings where unlike any of the others; both times I sat amazed as he spoke about his life and how he had a completely new reference point. I'm reminded of the verse, all is of God, old things of man are passed away and behold, and all things are new, 2 Corinthians 5:17. I could see in him and hear in his words how he connected in a union with the Lord and had begun a transformation, becoming a new creation, one who had never before existed.

As you read this, I know you know what this means.

So I asked him, what are you doing? As in, "Did you find the answer to, Now What?"

He replied, "Nothing."

He said the continuing enlightenment of the scriptures and his progressively seeing himself more clearly as spirit man gave him greater capacity to see the Father as well. It is a self perpetuating process.

We spoke about the changes in his family, changes which just seemed to happen without his or any other person's involvement. Decisions became clear and family issues began to resolve with no effort. To summarize, He and his family are flourishing. They're not the only ones either.

Another friend wrote this, "Something has happened to me; a settling in me, a determination to be above this place. Not to be pious but to be called out and separated from this atmosphere. There is an existence built for us that is separate from the physical boundaries or sin. We are the fruit of the Vine and therefore products of His life."

Jesus said He came to give us an abundant life. We decided on our own that we should work for it, to our detriment.

We will never qualify ourselves for living as spirit man in union with the Lord. He wants to grace us, as a gift, with a new existence and with a new awareness of our union. Then we will perceive the spirit realm where He is clearly seen by His children and the result will be we will love Him and He will do the following for us:

Deuteronomy 11:21,
That your days may be multiplied, and the days of your children, in the land which the Lord swore unto your fathers to give them, *as the days of heaven upon the earth* KJV

Considering all the people I know who've had an eye opening experience as described above, all the basic elements in their stories are the same, mine included. The similar framework of events and effects is striking and the effortless rich, abundant fruit continues. Their very first comment tells of a new way of looking at their world, their life and peace begins to settle in and the sense of fragmentation leaves.

The main point you need to realize is this; the spirit man exists as light or darkness based on the decision a person makes about Jesus. Once a choice is made in favor of Him and what's written of Him is believed to be true, the Life of Jesus causes the rebirth and the eyes of the spirit man are opened, it is a literal resurrection of the spirit of the individual.

Look at what Paul told the Philippians in 3:10-11, that I may know Him, and the power (flowing out) of His resurrection, and the fellowship of His sufferings (as a spirit man limited by the physical body), becoming conformed unto His death (thus being transformed into His likeness); 11) if by any means I may attain unto the resurrection (of the spirit man I am) from the dead (even while in the body). ASV

If we pursue educating ourselves with the ultimate goal to please God, by way of our lofty education, the blinders slowly cover the once clear vision. We end up in worse shape than before, bound by our own flavor of religion regardless of church attendance. Freedom is again lost and we paralyze ourselves with self judgment and self demeaning opinions.

For me, once I saw I am His son and if a son then as spirit I am eternal just like God, I realized the perfect work Jesus did is also made perfect in me as spirit and this condition does not change unless I make another choice opposed to the one I currently believe about the Lord. In other words, regardless of my conduct or behavior, the condition of the spirit man doesn't change. BUT, if my conduct is not conducive or consistent with the character or personality of Jesus, there's a problem. Jesus said we're known by our fruit, what we do which is seen and experienced by others. Our life flows from the spirit, what we do reveals the condition of what we are as spirit man. This flowing is an ongoing and unstoppable force from the heart, spirit/soul. The effect is the life and existence to which we are now subject. We allow ourselves success in relation to what we believe about ourselves; this is the way of the world and is opposed to us as children of the living God.

We disjoint and fragment our self and establish the same in relation to Him.

I listen to all manner of conversation about the things of God, sermons of ministers included. In most every conversation their words reveal only a sense of separation or disjointing as individuals. Because of this, their message instills the sense of isolation from the Lord, Who is our Source, and leaves people thinking they need Him to "come do this or that for me." Listen carefully and you will hear the isolated individual being addressed and the information only instills more isolation. We too often think the Lord should come to us on our behalf. On the other hand, Jesus said it was the Father within Him Who did the work, in terms of our lives; we should now bear the same witness.

Here is Paul's testimony of this same experience about his life as written to the Ephesians:

Ephesians 4:17-24,
This I say therefore, and testify in the Lord, that you no longer walk as the Gentiles (outsiders) also walk, in the vanity (futility and folly) of their mind, 18) being darkened in their understanding, alienated (estranged and self banished) from the life of God, because of the ignorance (lack of spirit perception) that is in them, because of the hardening of their heart (and the feeling of estrangement); 19) who being past feeling (and apathetic) gave themselves up to lasciviousness (unbridled indulgence and impurity), to work all uncleanness with greediness (having an attitude inclined toward all types of impurities)(thus demonstrating their lack of spirit perception and reality).

20) But you did not so learn Christ;

21) if so be that you heard Him, and were taught by Him, even as truth is in Jesus: 22) that you put away (by stripping yourself), as concerning your former manner of life, the old man, that grows corrupt after the lusts of deceit (of a deluded mind which cannot perceive the spirit realm); 23) and that you be (constantly) renewed in the spirit of your mind, 24) and put on the

new (spirit) man, that after (the image of) God has been created in righteousness and holiness of (and rooted in) truth. ASV

I testify in having this experience I'm writing about, I'm no longer aware of a separation between me and the Lord, instead I'm attentive to my union with Him, by the Holy Spirit. Our two lives have been made to be one, a union is formed which He maintains. I no longer feel excluded due to my failures, He cleanses me and I reside in a perfect union with Him within this body I live in. I know He wants good for me now and when I take on the perspective of a perfect son I do not consider myself excluded or disqualified so I fully expect all the good He has for me, I'm blessed.

The term blessing, which is used so much in church circles, is vitally different now as you can see. The blessing of the Lord, which He wants us to possess and experience, exists on the spirit level. It's an empowerment He bestows only to the spirit man, a result of the two now being together as one. If there are manifestations which appear as a result of the union, we may fail to see the spirit source because we are distracted by the physical event. So the things in life we consider good and therefore a blessing, they are only the results of the real blessing to us from Daddy, cause He can't help Himself.

This new spirit man is stable in all his ways as compared to James 1:8 saying the double minded man is unstable in all his ways. One aspect of double mindedness is learning biblical facts or religious rituals and thereby hoping to attain some level of the spirit life and/or pleasing God. This effort is based on a deep level of deception because a person in this condition cannot even recognize spirit. The Bible is a collection of spirit inspired words which leads man to a spirit life. The double mindedness develops when the intended effect is not achieved and the person tries to live by the content of their mind with no substance as spirit for support.

Here's my conclusion so far, if you're reading this wanting new information to fit into your current, new frame of mind, forget it. You are already drifting off track and headed for a ditch.

Yes we pray, read scriptures and spend time focused on the Lord and ourselves in fellowship, this means giving thought to ourselves in this "new to us" reality and seeing what we are and all things which accompany this wholeness condition. We do the same things for much different reasons. Daddy wants to have a direct relationship with no need of His children teaching each other, Hebrews 8:11.

Here is all you really need to know; with the eyes of the spirit man now open, the experience thus far is your pattern. Continue therein with no distractions. This is a self perpetuating process led by the Holy Spirit.

3
UNITY

We were not designed to function as isolated individuals. The entirety of our relationship is clearly shown and proven in the Bible, and is identified as a family in a perfect union. Jesus did prove this by saying He and His Father are One, a perfect union in all things.

When I give thought to this relationship, I know there is no thing which can separate us from Him. Nothing!

The promised rest and inward reflection held over till now for the faithful, just as Elohiym rested and reflected on the seventh day of creation, is now settling in you, and you know it!

You might think of this better as satisfaction which prompts no further actions.

This is a new existence. One of becoming acquainted with "being," one described as having extreme wellness. This is a life form shown in the Bible to be spirit, existing in the image and likeness of the Creators. The spirit man is an eternal spirit being but overall we do not think of ourselves this way. The "being" of man cannot be possessed by man, his intellect or his body, so we can no longer refer to "my spirit." The Bible says we're not our own but have been bought with a price so the Supreme Being Himself owns us in every respect. Yet, He has given us the heritage of an heir to Him and made us joint heirs with Jesus. He says He adopted us as His own children so now we call Him "Abba," Aramaic to this day for Daddy.

What is "being"? This "being" is spirit, so what is spirit? God is Spirit (John 4:24) but spirit is not God. Jesus said in John 6:63, "It is the spirit that gives life; the flesh profits nothing: the words that I have spoken unto you are spirit, and are life." ASV

The nature of spirit can be seen by the outward fruit which Paul told the Galatians is Love, Joy, Peace, Patience, Kindness, Goodness, Faithfulness, Gentleness, and Self-control. These things are the image and likeness of Elohiym, our Father. Nothing can oppose these nor compare, they exist in absolute life and they are timeless expressions of the spirit personality. Meditate a bit here, in heaven, now or later, your ultimate "being" will be described by the traits on this list. You will not do them, you will be them, remember the Bible tells us God IS Love, as will you. Here is clarity of the perfect union.

Consider this, what you are is spirit. Who you are is a unique combination of the fruit of the spirit shown forth as a forever one-of-a-kind representation of your Father as your Source. Again, Jesus is our case in point, our model or pattern. When Elohiym made you He "threw away the mold," no other person can take your place and fulfill the purpose you possess. Your mind cannot define or even grasp this state of being.

What does this mean to you now? Was Jesus successful? Did He ever fail? Did He fear? He knew Himself as Spirit. Consider how His example could actually be your unique experience as a result of the work of the Holy Ghost. Do we have to wait until after we die to begin to live, naturally showing forth these nine traits? Why wait? What will be the response? You get extravagant fulfillment which gives Him glory.

The physical body of man is flesh but flesh is not always man, sometimes it is animal and is essentially different compared to man. I want to set up a mindset for you to properly discern our relationship to Daddy. By seeing Him as equivalent or comparable life forms we also get a glimpse of what we are and by seeing Jesus we learn what we can be, the outcome of your being unified through Him and with Him.

Adam and Eve were unified with Him but became isolated; their death was the result of being forsaken, excluded individual beings who chose to change covenants and gods. We are now individuals whose purpose is to show forth His Excellencies but in the rest and union upheld by the Holy Spirit. This isn't two beings in one body, this is two beings joined in union into one existence and one expression.

This is very difficult to understand mentally but we have a great example recorded in the Gospels where the life of the Son of man/Son of God is demonstrated. We are to be like Him by way of His power.

I don't know when I began to have the following desire but I have for years asked of the Lord for me to know what it is to be His son. I'm serious; I want to know what it means and whatever experience goes with it. I still want to know but I never guessed this eye opening would happen.

Back in the early 1980's a friend gave me a business card with the following printed on it:

One side said, Jeremiah 33:3,
"Call unto Me and I will answer you and show you great and mighty things that you know not of."

Side two says, "Take this prayer which is an adaptation of Ephesians 1:17-19 and make it your own – many times a day until your being is saturated with it. You will find a new world opening up to you.

'Father, give me a spirit of wisdom and of revelation in the knowledge of the Lord Jesus Christ.

I pray that the eyes of my heart may be enlightened, flooded with light, so that I may know and realize the hope to which You have called me … the riches of the glory of Your inheritance in me … what is the surpassing greatness of Your power that is now mine – the very same power that raised Christ from the dead and exalted Him to heaven and now made over to me.

Open my eyes this day and lead me into being who I am in Christ, Amen.'"

I did this for years. I was, at the time, so caught up in church and teaching classes and wanting the ministry for myself I could see nothing else for me. I didn't know anyone who lived in the spirit dimension who could coach me. We all did the same thing, we studied, prayed and attended church, nothing wrong but nothing much happened. We had little to offer but a promise, the ultimate promise of heaven for sure. The unspoken attitude seemed to be, "We are going to have a lot of trouble in life just like everyone else but at least we will go to heaven."

I went to a church meeting in August 1999 where the preacher, who I hadn't seen before or since, looked at me and said to me this prayer almost word for word. He said the Lord was taking me into an area of sonship I had asked Him for. Afterward, nothing happened except a painful process of purging, but He did the work in me. If I tried to do for myself, what only the Lord could do, as I hope you will not, it would have ruined me.

Carnal man can't operate in this realm of spirit which the Bible calls the Kingdom of God. He's detached. The methods of the world and the kingdom are not the same.

Spiritual knowledge is very dangerous if not handled by us as spirit man with the help of the Holy Spirit! Stop here and think!

If you're finding the urge to "do this prayer" hoping to help your transformation I urge to ask yourself why. Can you really help anything in this process? Your purest motive for this is simply your clear desire to have what He says is yours. You do as Jesus said, consider the life of the birds and flowers and take no thought for tomorrow.

The words I've written can do nothing. Only the Lord can open our eyes and do this work of completion. This is true for the Bible as well. The writers of the biblical text wrote from experience, faithfulness and what they saw from their point of reference as spirit. The Holy Spirit is said to have borne them along and inspired them but not as in dictation of something strange to them. If they did not have this reality within them, then whatever they may have written was just hearsay and guess work. Instead, the spirit man you are will now see the cohesive message from cover to cover.

Only in this sprit realm or dimension can apparent individuals be one in existence and purpose yet be a distinct, unique revelation of the Father. The problem in the formula is our inability to occupy our place, prepared by Jesus, because we don't think like this and we can't see the Truth on our own. Again, for an example take a look at what we have recorded in the Gospels about Jesus. The Lord gave us a perfect example of the life He wants us to have. Don't think you can do the things He did for the public but focus on Him personally as your personal pattern. What was His personal life like? Did He fear disease, or demons, nature or other men? Was He anxious or did He question God?

If you are having trouble with these ideas please don't close your mind. If you do, the Lord may be unable for some time to clearly show you what He wants, I don't imply you will ever agree, but you might.

4
DEFINE YOUR NEW WORLD

Seeing your Father clearly shows you what and who you are. You "look" just like Him and He gave you everything you need to reign as a king in your sphere of influence. Here you must learn to recognize your dwelling place and how to bring about His will. Jesus showed us how.

Romans 12:1-2,
1) I beseech (implore) you therefore, brethren, by (or in view of) the (obvious) mercies of God, to present your bodies a living sacrifice (which has no mind of its own), holy, acceptable to God, (which is) your spiritual service.

2) And be not fashioned (conformed) according to this world: but be transformed by the renew-

ing of your mind, that you may prove what is the good and acceptable and perfect will of God. ASV

I want to rephrase what Paul wrote to the Roman church but speak directly to you.

Verse 1) Considering the tremendous and wonderful mercy the Lord has clearly shown you in all He has done through Jesus in order to restore to you the spirit element of "being", you should freely and willing offer your body to Him in service as a living sacrifice. In doing so, you will demonstrate how the spirit man has risen to his rightful place of dominance and command both individually and also in respect to the total creation. This will be your ordained place of full and complete service to Him since you are now more capable to relate to Daddy and therefore more capable to represent Him.

Verse 2) In this position don't any longer allow yourself to be molded or fashioned to the world system, but instead stay focused on allowing an unhindered process of transformation, a true metamorphosis, whereby the spirit man will gradually be established in your life as planned from the beginning. This is the only course of action which will enable you to prove His will as just described and show its very completion as acceptable, good in the purest sense and perfect as He desires for you.

Conformity to the world system is forever our enemy. The Lord created us to be individuals, each one able to uniquely represent His magnificent attributes and character traits to all. He wants us to see Him in each other and marvel at the wonder of His wisdom and love. This idea isn't new because we can do this now as we look at the life of Jesus and consider Him. He said Himself; if you have seen Me you have seen the Father. In this respect and at some point in history there will exist a people on the earth who are the mighty generation spoken of by the prophets. I believe they will be the last generation of the dispensation of grace and people will say of them as in Acts, they have been with Jesus.

So how does conformity appear?

Sure you will act and dress like others who are members of your group but at the same time you know inside you don't fit nor belong there. You may think everything they stand for is fulfilling and offers security but they know as well, in the end, the culture is not going to deliver.

You are a product of your environment. Well meaning family, friends, colleagues, etc. shaped you in their image and likeness, without spirit considerations.

The process of conformity is the same as described in Romans 12, you set out to learn the doctrine of the group and you parroted, studied and learned it until you were changed from the inside out. You began to talk like them and act like them until you became accepted. The unspoken intent of their creed is to keep you in compliance. You will be unpopular and shunned if you don't comply. You may be happy for a while but conformity holds a shallow promise in light of the vast individuality we were purposed to express.

Emerson said conformity is equal to suicide. We must realize the Creators are infinite personalities and created us to be as such. True freedom releases a person to fully be themselves as created in the image and likeness of Elohiym. You and I are the warden of the prison we created for ourselves; Jesus came to set captives free. Free from whom? Ourselves!

Without the involvement of spirit there can be no true purpose. The world seeks purpose and fulfillment but it can't produce it. Once again we see how the world system creates a problem and offers a good looking, desirable but useless solution. The futility only deepens man's emptiness.

Man continues to do the same thing over and over but the results are always the same. This can be called insanity but it's also the only offer out there in the world. We need what is real; we need to discover ourselves as designed by the Creators.

Accepting restoration of ourselves to original intent is described biblically as redemption which is the concept of buying back a possession once owned by the redeemer. It means to release by paying a ransom price.

Think about Peter's report,
1 Peter 1:13-21,
Therefore gird up the loins of your mind, be sober, and rest your hope fully upon the grace that is to be brought to you at the revelation of Jesus Christ; 14) as obedient children, not conforming yourselves to the former lusts, as in your ignorance; 15) but as He who called you is holy, you also be holy in all your conduct, 16) because it is written, "Be holy, for I (God) am holy."

When we see Him we shall be like Him but not by any effort on our part. This is for the spirit man now, in this life. We can't do holiness; notice the Lord says to BE holy as He is. It is the state of "being." If you don't know you're a spirit man this verse can't apply with success.

17) And if you call on the Father, who without partiality judges according to each one's work (because the work reveals its spirit source), conduct yourselves throughout the time of your stay here in (respect) fear (this is a direct reference to spirit as staying here on earth); 18) knowing that you were not redeemed with corruptible things, like silver or gold, from your aimless conduct (without spiritual direction) received by tradition from your fathers, 19) but with the precious blood of Christ, as of a lamb without blemish and without spot. 20) He indeed was foreordained before the foundation (casting down) of the world, but was manifest in these last times for you 21) who through Him believe in God, who raised Him from the dead and gave Him glory, so that your faith and hope are in God.

So how will your stay here be, in your world?

More of the same? Like it says in Hebrews?

Hebrews 6:4-6,
For as touching (or concerning) those who were once enlightened (as spirit man) and tasted of the heavenly gift, and were made partakers of the Holy Spirit, 5) and tasted the good (living) word of God, and the powers of the age to come, 6) and (then) fell away, it is impossible to renew them again unto repentance; seeing they crucify

to themselves the Son of God afresh, and put Him to an open shame. ASV

Important changes are taking place, we need to know what are the new responsibilities. This falling away is from the realm of the spirit man and his place in the kingdom with Daddy. If we neglect our place and have no respect thereof, this verse could apply to those who know the subject we are discussing but abandon it.

What about the above list?
1. Enlightened
2. Tasted the heavenly gift
3. Partakers of the Holy Spirit
4. Tasted the Living Word of God
5. Tasted the powers of the age to come

Enlightened – Proverbs 4:18 the path of a righteous man is like a (light of brightness). From the Hebrew word Naga

Tasted – Psalms 34:9 Taste and see that God is good. Taste = Experience, from the Hebrew word Taam

Partakers – Used as a phrase in Joshua 22:27 as a right or privilege in YHWH, (Jehovah), Hebrews 4:4 …and it was given to them as right or privilege in the Holy Spirit

Tasted the Living Word of God – And have experienced the good promises of God and the powers of the coming world. Isaiah 40:29-31

Who are these for? This we do know. They are not for any man who falls away and whose renewal unto repentance becomes impossible. When is the time for repentance? Now, while we are in the body. So, the items on the list can be ours now as a whole man. Each item is to be experienced as a result of the spirit union we now have. Our "being" has literally changed.

You are in the world but not of it.

So, according to the resulting condition of a person who experienced the five things listed, how would you judge their prospects for success in life? Would you consider the answer to be as good as Jesus?

Having dominion restored, man can now shape his world, his life experience through these five things and more. How will this look?

You will no longer be a victim of circumstances which would be considered good or bad. You will see and live in a real place right now. Love, peace, joy, kindness, etc. will be your stable experience regardless of what you see and hear about calamity. You define and shape your life now guided by the pattern Jesus offers. You impart what you possess to others without effort.

5
TRAINING

Having discovered what and who you are and how you are in your perfect union with Daddy and His purpose, a new life and way thereof can be experienced. The Gospels show us how Jesus lived with Him intimately for an example to show us what we can have with Him now. Hebrews 13:8 says He is the same yesterday, today and forever. Paul wrote in several letters how we are to grow up into Christ in all things. He told the Galatians he travailed for them in prayer until Christ be formed in them.

Romans 6:4, 5, 8 - 11,
We were buried therefore with Him through (water) baptism unto death: that like as Christ was raised from the dead through the glory of

the Father, <u>so we also might walk (or conduct ourselves) in newness of life.</u> 5) For if we have become united with (Him) in the likeness of His death, we shall be also (in the likeness) of His resurrection (raised to a new life like His);

8) <u>But if we died with Christ, we believe that we shall also live with Him (forever including now);</u> 9) knowing that Christ being raised from the dead dies no more; death no more has dominion over Him. 10) For the death that He died, He died unto sin once: but the life that He lives, He lives unto God. 11) Even so (in the same way) reckon also yourselves to be dead unto sin, but alive unto God in Christ Jesus. ASV

The new existence requires training because we, like the children of Israel in the wilderness, still have an old, worldly mindset and way of thinking which is not favorable to submitting to the new spirit reality. Their old Egyptian mentality shut them out of the Promised Land although they were just miraculously delivered from slavery. The Lord actually waited for the Egyptian generation mentality to die off before He let the new generation into the promise. He even said, at the end of the forty years, Joshua and Caleb were of a different spirit.

Think a minute, consider what they saw and experienced and how the powerful external miraculous events didn't condition them to believe or to enter the promise and live with God. Without spirit oversight and discipline applied to our every thought, we too will fail to live in the abundance to which we now have access. We need training.

Training is discipleship (or schooling). Discipline is required because the old patterns of thought must change. The death in verse eight above is not physical or we could not live with Him in newness of life here on earth. The familiar way of life and way of thinking must be purged by the new man and his way of life in the kingdom system of government. This government is for authentic persons who know what they are and who they are. They may look and act the same but their source of life has switched from the mind alone, influenced by darkness, to the mind under the control of the recreated spirit man.

Don't be led astray by attempting actions alone before you become a person who would normally and naturally do them, especially related to this discipline. Your conduct must stand on the character and nature of the spirit man initiating and supporting it. Your behavior must flow from the heart as described by Proverbs 4:23.

Jesus told His disciples He had food to eat they knew not, John 4:32. Paul told the elders of

Ephesus in Acts 20:32, "So now, brethren, I commend you to God and to the word of His grace, which is able to build you up and give you an inheritance among all those who are sanctified." What is of man which needs building up? It's twofold, renewing the mind to new creation realities and edifying the spirit with Truth whereby you learn who you are in Christ. Thereby you occupy your place of dominion in your personal affairs. Your focus must be primarily on your condition of heart, the inseparable spirit/soul.

This is the taking of every thought captive but also a growing into living "now", which is a place of timelessness, a moment of neither past nor future. The spirit dimension is always now. Jesus said we are to take no thought for tomorrow; His blood has cleansed our past and future since He carried the sin of the whole world. Society in general avoids "now" because it proves we have no control and we fear the impending chaos. "Now" is our only place of contact with the Lord and the only place Truth applies; anyone who claims to speak Truth but in terms of the past or future is deceived.

Our "now" is uncomfortable because it reveals our human inadequacies as well. As long as we interfere with the spirit realm by our own actions to manipulate desired results we will fail to be in union with Him and nothing happens. For instance, prayer is taught in the context of how we can move God on our behalf but prayer is for us to represent His will alone, this implies the one who prays knows what is God's will and is in union. Consider "The Lord's Prayer" Jesus taught in this context. Whose will is to be done? Not ours, but God's.

God can only be found in the now, Jesus proved this. Your mind wants to fret over the past and cower in fear of the unknown future. Being distracted in this manner will prevent the vital real-time union which sustains you. It will interpret your circumstances and judge you inadequate to succeed and victimize you every time. The spirit man is not a victim but Paul told the Romans you are to reign as a king in life through Jesus.

Never once can it be found where Jesus walked or functioned anywhere but in His present chaotic reality. Never once did He tell a person you aren't good enough or you should or shouldn't have done this or that, dealing with past or future. Instead He connected and brought to bear the will of the Father with compassion and power.

When you mature this passage will be clear: Philippians 2:5-8,

Have this mind in you, which was also in Christ Jesus: 6) Who, existing in the form of God, counted not the being on an equality with God a thing to be grasped, 7) but emptied Himself (took off the garment of Kingship), taking the form of a servant, being made in the likeness of men; 8) and being found in fashion as a man, He humbled Himself (as Spirit), becoming obedient (even) unto death, yes, the death of the cross. ASV

When you look at the life of Jesus in the Gospels you see a man, as described above, Who knew He is spirit and what it means. He is the example given to all who want to be fulfilled and satisfied, existing in the particular rest held over for those faithful to the union. Rest is a type of self sufficiency belonging to spirit beings created in the likeness and image of Elohiym.

Would you dare to let this mind be in you?

Would you dare to take your hands off your life and trust Him as Daddy? Will you allow Him to show you this isn't about what you have for Him but what He has for you? Can you realize you have nothing to offer and you will never qualify but He has you covered?

The following verses must be viewed as your present spirit reality. Don't create a list of things to do. I'm saying this knowing you now see but I also know your mind will want something to do to get control.

James 1:22-25,
But (from the spirit) be doers of the word and not hearers only, deluding your own selves. 23) For if any one is a hearer of the word and not a doer, he is like unto a man beholding his natural face in a mirror: 24) for he beholds himself, and goes away, and straightway (or quickly) forgets what manner of man he was (even what he looks like). 25) But he that looks into the perfect law, the (law) of liberty, and (so) continues, being not a hearer that forgets but a doer that works, this man shall be blessed in his doing (because he has seen what and who he is). ASV

2 Corinthians 3:16-18,
But whenever (a person) shall turn to the Lord, the veil is taken away. 17) Now the Lord is the Spirit: and where the Spirit of the Lord is, (there) is liberty. 18) But we all (as spirit), with unveiled face beholding as in a mirror the glory of the Lord (as we see Him we see ourselves), are transformed into the same image from (one degree or level of) glory to glory, even as from the Lord the Spirit. ASV Read this whole passage in the Bible.

1 Timothy 4:15,

Be diligent in these things; give yourself wholly to them; that your progress (growth) may be manifest unto all. ASV

Philippians 4:8,
Finally, brethren, whatever things are true, whatever things are honorable, whatever things are just, whatever things are pure, whatever things are lovely, whatever things are of good report; if there be any virtue (in terms of the sustaining life force), and if there be any praise, think on these things. ASV Biblical mind control.

Joshua 1:8,
This book of the law shall not depart out of your mouth, but you shall meditate thereon day and night, that you may observe to do according to all that is written therein: for then you shall make your way prosperous, and then you shall have good success. ASV

Psalms 1:2-3,
But his delight is in the law of Jehovah; and on His law does he meditate day and night. 3) And he shall be like a tree planted by the streams of water, that brings forth its fruit in its season, whose leaf also does not wither; and whatever he does shall prosper. ASV

The Hebrew word for meditate means both to intently think on and to speak of. Speaking

Truth to yourself as part of a thinking process can be helpful. Set aside a time for mental stillness and concentration on the meaning of certain verses and their application while in the attitude of spirit as well as the spirit being as the point of reference. I know I can try to explain this dynamic and fail but with the effect of your now open eyes it won't matter because you will simply "get it." You will know you are being spoken to as a perfect spirit son and your thoughts will never cheat or rob you. This is the stability of which I speak.

The words on the pages of the Bible are meaningless until they are made alive to you in the spirit context where you will then receive an edification or "building up" of the real man. This event is mostly bit by bit and not dramatic. Don't fear Him. You will see a difference looking back six to twelve months in comparison.

Matthew 4:4,
Man shall not live by bread alone, but by every word which proceeds out from mouth of God.

1 John 3:21-24 says if your heart does not condemn you, you will have confidence toward God and whatever you ask of Him you will receive. Your heart will not condemn you when you stay focused on your true self as the result of the per-

fect work of the Spirit of Christ. Philippians 3:3-9 says you should have no confidence in the flesh. Where is the confidence to be placed but in your perfect union with Daddy?

I hope you are grasping the impact of your decision for the Lord and its far reaching, eternal effect on your person. This message will not give a place for guilt, fear or self condemnation which will separate you from Him and all He has for you. You will become His living letter written to everyone you know and meet but you benefit the most.

A summary may help you:
Set a time for learning to quiet all the noise of the rat race and its affect. How long doesn't matter.

Allow thoughts to remind you of being His son or daughter as spirit and He has made you perfect in Christ.

Be alert and write or record what you hear.

Expect to be led by the Holy Spirit 24/7.

6
SERVING IN SPIRIT

The training will never end unless we refuse to participate. Paul spoke in 2 Timothy 2:4 about while in military service the soldier is not to become entangled in civilian affairs. This is a spirit dynamic speaking of reaching a point in spiritual maturity where we no longer allow becoming victimized by our thoughts. Distractions we can't afford the deeper we move into our reasonable service.

But, we can't make the jump from being literally a babe in spirit to the "fully matured" in the Greek word used on Romans 8.

Galatians 3:24-4:1-7,

24) So that the law (our moral code) is become our tutor (to bring us) unto Christ, that we might be justified by faith (by believing and occupying our union in Him). 25) But now faith has arrived, we are no longer under a tutor. 26) For you are all sons of God, through faith, in Christ Jesus. 27) For as many of you as were baptized into Christ did put on Christ. 28) There can be neither Jew nor Greek (on a spirit level), there can be neither bond nor free, there can be no male and female; for you all are one (spirit) in Christ Jesus. 29) And if you are Christ's, then are you Abraham's seed, heirs according to promise (according to Abraham's covenant).

4:1) But I say that so long as the heir is a child, he differs nothing from a bondservant (slave) though he is lord of all; 2) but is under guardians and stewards until the day appointed of the father. 3) So we also, when we were children, were held in bondage under the fundamentals of the world: 4) but when the fullness of the time came, God sent forth his Son, born of a woman, born under the law, 5) that He might redeem them that were under the law, that we might receive the adoption of sons. 6) And because you are sons, God sent forth the Spirit of his Son into our hearts, crying, Abba, (Aramaic to this day for "Daddy") Father. 7) So that you are no longer a bondservant, but a son; and if a son, then an heir through God. ASV THIS IS GOOD NEWS!

Until you learn to live and function within the spirit realm your current method of operation must continue, including in particular, you must adhere to your moral code. People respond everyday to each event dictated by their dual moral standards of right and wrong. This is a belief system taught from birth by your guardians. These things at best are imprinted on the mind to control the fallen nature with which you have been born. This type of life can appear to be right and is socially acceptable and you operate daily without much thought. Now, though you are a child of God, you are kept and guarded by the law or moral code until you grow into a mature son, neither male nor female.

This is a new way of looking at things.

Since we've been the product and a citizen of the world's spirit system we couldn't function in God's kingdom spirit system. Now we're given the opportunity and made able to move our citizenship to another spirit system, the kingdom of God. We function in the world as a soul and body combination, Paul defined this with the Greek term "sarx." It describes the person who is by nature not inclined toward the spirit being he is, at all. His mind is a dictator and out of control.

NT:4561
(sarx); the body as the symbol of what is external, or human nature with its weaknesses and fleshly tendencies, or explicitly a human being.

Romans 7:5-6,
For when we were in the flesh, the sinful passions, which were (aroused) through the law, worked in our (bodily) members to bring forth fruit unto death. 6 But now we have been discharged from the law, having died to that (law) wherein we were held; so that we serve in newness of the spirit, and not in oldness (or old ways) of the letter. ASV

When you settle into the spirit perspective you'll realize the power of the Bible as words which are spirit and life. It is spiritually discerned for those who possess the Holy Spirit, your Guide and Teacher.

1 Corinthians 2:14-3:4,
Now the natural man receives not the things of the Spirit of God: for they are foolishness unto him; and he cannot know them, because they are spiritually judged (discerned). 15) But he that is spiritual (from the spirit perspective) judges all things, and he himself is judged of no man. 16) For who has known the mind of the Lord, that

he should instruct Him? But we have the mind of Christ.

3:1) And I, brethren, could not speak unto you as unto spiritual (from the spirit perspective), but as unto carnal, as unto babes in Christ. 2) I fed you with milk, not with meat; for you were not yet able (to bear it): no, not even now are you able; 3) for you are yet carnal (and fleshly): for whereas (as long as) there is among you jealousy and strife (or any other fruit of the flesh nature), are you not carnal, and do you not walk after the manner of men (in the flesh)? 4) For when one says, I am of Paul; and another, I am of Apollos; are you not (mere) men (as opposed to another type of man)? ASV

Is the claiming of their favorite minister the only thing which made them carnal? No, they were carnal to start with and the division of themselves into groups under the labels defined by those who minister among them was the outward appearance of the origin of their actions.

In contrast, remember Jesus was about thirty years of age when He started His work which we read about. Even His service developed over time. If Jesus had no true knowledge of Himself individually, how would He ever have wrapped His mind around being the Savior of the world?

Your service to the Lord is first and foremost to yourself as His child. By offering yourself to Him, the Holy Spirit can begin His work to mold you into the image of Christ and grow you up into Him in all things. You must mature as spirit man, male or female, but this maturity will allow no distinctions. This real existence is the true foundation for life in all things having to do with creation as it longs for the disclosure of the mature sons of Elohiym, Romans 8.

His opening our eyes to the spirit realm and our occupation thereof is only a first step in this birthing process but will lead us to serve Him out of what He has done for us.

Luke 1:80,
And the child (Jesus) grew, and became strong in spirit, and was in the deserts till the day of His showing unto Israel. ASV

Romans 7:6,
But now we have been discharged from the law, having died to that wherein we were held; so that we serve in newness of the spirit, and not in oldness of the letter. ASV

7
GROWING UP

What is not growing is dying, or at least dormant. You must get beyond your comfort zone. The Bible says nothing is impossible to him who believes. Once we achieve the first level of impossibility there will logically be the next one. Progress in maturity must continue as you give attention to the new spirit life and the kingdom system of government where you will now function. This concept of uninterrupted development will offend your mind, thankfully.

Does a goal exist with a pattern to guide us? Yes.

Acts 11:26,
… and it came to pass, that even for a whole year they were gathered together with the church,

and taught much people, and that the disciples were called Christians first in Antioch. ASV

Acts 4:13,
Now when they beheld the boldness of Peter and John, and had perceived that they were unlearned and ignorant men (in terms of the rabbinic discipline taught in their schools), they marveled; and they took knowledge of them, that they had been with Jesus. ASV

Christians at first were recognized to have been with Jesus, not just Peter and John, they set the example. Read Acts in your new light. Yes, they were with Jesus, but they looked just like Him in character and behavior, do you?

What if *you* are the only Jesus you will ever see? Think about it, where else would He be found for you? Again, you are to be molded into His image. For who? You first for sure!

What do we have when we come to Him?

The life I have right now came from within me. I created it without Him and it includes an identity I have assumed. It is "the mind made self" the Bible calls the old man. The mind made person is false or counterfeit and will never be fulfilled, therefore he is always needy. Your being convinced you know who you are will set your attention on continuing to build up the person you are. This will be blinding to any open minded-ness which would allow information capable to expand the boundaries.

I have some of what I want but not all. The reason for not having everything I want, a very modest list, is, until recently I have judged my-self in light of my weaknesses and set limits, so some of the things I want for my life are out of my reach. I even suspect I have sabotaged some of my efforts because I would find myself in a strange new arena in life if a higher success were realized; a presumed uncomfortable situation socially because everyone I know right now is just like me. This applies.

I am becoming brutally honest with myself but have learned not to be condemning. Also, I have learned, the greatest obstacle in my life is what I think I know, so, I don't trust myself. This is healthy from the spirit perspective and deadly otherwise. I say this because the Holy Spirit will support and guard us as we gradually chan-geover from the old way to the new. Trying to "empty one's self" in any other way will be de-structive.

Do you know people who do things which cause you to say, "How do they do that?" They won-der how you do what you do as well. You are endowed with talents form the Creators. Enough talent to more than supply your every need with abundance.

I am a builder; I construct buildings for residential and commercial use. Every project I bring to completion started with an idea. This work fits me and I like real estate development. I see the detail at the beginning and work in more details as we build. No one can take this ability from me but I can, for numerous reasons, lay it down and quit. The only true, stable wealth in existence is within people, you included.

I am a business man; as such I look for talent to create a team to operate a company. The talent must complement my weaknesses and allow me to plan the future as an entrepreneur. I discover and develop talent and the related wealth. The blueprint I build by is my vision and tells the story for why we are here, in business and how we do things. I create a safe environment for people to become their best.

Our human insight is limited. Paul wrote in 2 Corinthians 5, we should no longer relate to each other physically but now in the new relationship of unity as spirit beings in harmony, the old way of looking at life has literally passed away. This new life and its perspective comes as a free gift from the Lord.

This next verse is a complete description of your new condition but needs to be considered from the newly enlightened spirit.

2 Timothy 1:7,
For God gave us not a spirit of fearfulness; but of power and love and discipline (of the mind and thoughts). ASV

The Creators have endowed the spirit realm with infinite resources. This is true for no other reason than YHWH, Jehovah, fills and upholds all things. Like the prodigal son, we have access at all times to infinite reserves. We have thus far wasted time in a rebellious lifestyle as citizens of the world system and since we have not occupied our Father's house the resources were not available. We can return at any time.

Jesus gave us an example when He sent Peter fishing, his profession, to get tax money for the Lord and himself. Remember, he found the money in the fish's mouth. We don't need this type of miracle, we should discover the talents and abilities we are abundantly given and concentrate on their development. The world tells us to work on our weaknesses, out of fear, to be current in the marketplace. We fear our faults and ignore our strengths; this does not apply in the Lord's economy.

The term "spirit of fearfulness" means the spirit man which is God given, doesn't originate, exist in nor produce fear. What does he look like? He consists of "dunamis," dynamo power, love and he brings discipline to the mind so it will yield and serve Him. This idea of discipline is the same written to the Romans as being renewed and directed in its service. So the spirit man brings to bear fearlessness, power and discipline upon the mind/emotions so it serves in the kingdom of Light.

By now you probably realize the entire Bible should be reread and rethought in new light. One aspect of this light is seeing the message from cover to cover is cohesive and not disjointed. The apparent confusion originates in a mental approach to a spirit message.

Someday this statement will not be necessary because the Lord's people will know even more about life in the spirit dimension.

8
KINGDOM REALITIES

I want to record various individual thoughts in this last chapter which will shed light on this new existence. You and I have such an indescribable opportunity in this era.

Matthew 6:31-34,
Be not therefore anxious, saying, what shall we eat? Or, what shall we drink? Or, Wherewithal shall we be clothed? 32) For after all these things do the Gentiles (the rest of the world) seek; for your heavenly Father knows that you have need of all these things.

33) But you seek first His kingdom (His spirit realm), and His righteousness (and your place of occupation in it); and all these things shall be

added unto you. 34 Be not therefore anxious for tomorrow: for tomorrow will be anxious for itself. Sufficient unto the day is the evil thereof. ASV

Luke 12:32,
Fear not, little flock; for it is your Father's good pleasure to give you the kingdom. ASV

This reminds me of the story about Mary and Martha, who wanted to serve Him, but Mary, wanted to hear and experience Him by sitting at the Lord's feet as He taught. We are mostly like Martha but now we can be like Mary and respond in kind, in spirit. This verse also shows how Jesus wanted us to focus on today's now. The main detractor of life as a spirit son is the pressures of life. See also the parable of the Sower where the types of ground show the effects the pressures of life can have on us as spirit.

Matthew 13:37-40,
He answered and said to them: "He who sows the good seed is the Son of Man. 38) The field is the world, the good seeds are the sons of the kingdom, but the tares are the sons of the wicked one. 39) The enemy who sowed them is the devil, the harvest is the end of the age, and the reapers are the angels. NKJV

Find everything you can to expand your thinking as a son in Him. You are a good seed! The Son of Man is the sower of the good seed! The term "seed" is used a lot to demonstrate the operation of the kingdom dimension. Jesus directly said the kingdom is like a seed and follows a similar growth process as does man.

###

Luke 8:10,
And He said, Unto you it is given to know the mysteries of the kingdom of God: but to the rest in parables; that seeing they may not see, and hearing they may not understand. ASV

I included this one because I refer to "seeing" so much. I don't want to use the term, "understanding," which may imply we should or could understand the spirit kingdom, we can't. We can see far more than we can understand and we can have all we see. We may grasp some ideas about it but with His help we can live far more of the infinite domain.

###

Luke 17:20-21,
And being asked by the Pharisees when the kingdom of God comes, He answered them and

said, The kingdom of God comes not with observation: 21) neither shall they say, Look, here! Or, there! Look, the kingdom of God is within you. ASV

Don't ever think these things are stored in a remote place in relation to you. There is no division established on God's part, you only need to enter into what He has for you. All this time I have told you about the kingdom, I referred to what you freely possess, regardless of your knowledge level. Remember Jesus said those who will enter the kingdom will do so as a little child. This infers innocence, trust and simplicity.

1 Corinthians 4:20,
For the kingdom of God is not in word, but in power. ASV

1 Corinthians 15:50,
Now this I say, brethren, that flesh and blood cannot inherit the kingdom of God; neither does corruption inherit incorruption. ASV

The physical and intellectual man is corruptible man and cannot inherit the kingdom. We can't put this inheritance off after our physical death, if we don't inherit now while we wait for going to heaven, we could miss out. The death creating this inheritance is the one Jesus experienced on our behalf.

Don't you think the world is waiting for a people to arise and demonstrate the power of His life so everyone would recognize Him?

Ephesians 5:18,
… but be filled with the Spirit; ASV

Hebrew verbs are aspects related to actions, they continue until the action is recorded to stop. The term "be filled" is one describing an uninterrupted, lifelong cramming full to the max of the Spirit infused existence. This means your attention becomes fixed on another realm, one which is real and true where you can live daily. The original words for "spirit" are very generic. Translation to indicate the type of spirit is based on context unless the wording is specific and says what kind of spirit is intended. In this verse, context is relied upon and could include the idea of the new creation man as well. This applies to your new life, very good news for you.

So, it could read, "… be filled and keep on being filled with the Holy Spirit." Continuous or uninterrupted infilling is required for us to live out the full potential He has given us.

After Jesus arose and met the disciples, He instructed them to wait in Jerusalem until they were endued with power from on high. He referred to the arrival of the Holy Spirit in power, infusing the spirit man of His followers. This event, in varying degrees must happen to Christians today. I'm not pushing any other manifestations, such as speaking in tongues, while the body of Christ is wanting of the fruit as explained in Galatians 5.

Anyone who thrives in spirit will be characterized by abundant and rich fruit, the greatest of them all is Love in the absolute, offered without qualification, restriction, opposition, requirement, expectation, judgment, criticism, repayment or fear.

Mark 4:21-25,
And He (Jesus) said unto them, Is the lamp brought to be put under the bushel, or under the bed, (and) not to be put on the stand? 22 For there is nothing hid, save that it should be manifested; neither was (anything) made secret, but that it should come to light. 23 If any man has ears to hear, let him hear. 24 And he said unto them, Take heed what you hear: with what measure you use it shall be measured unto you; and more shall be given unto you. 25 For he that

has, to him shall be given: and he that has not, from him shall be taken away even that which he has. ASV

The spirit man is the lamp of the body and Jesus is making a direct reference to the spirit man brought forth to occupy his prominent place. In his place, spirit words will be heard by the intellect and a measurement of validity will be applied. Either the intellect will dismiss or diminish the message or allow it full access and effect. This applies to any source of any report. When our point of reference to judge the report is the reality of the spirit man, his light reveals the Truth. Jesus allows us to see our real self in His light and His reality; we then take hold of a true standard for guidance. This is good; the possibility of eliminating mistakes is available.

The practical application is this, everyday you will hear reports from others who declare their opinion concerning you as a person or your circumstances. Regardless of their intent to help you or not, you will then judge the validity of the report and how it affects you. A good example is your doctor. The doc is a recognized and trusted professional which you trust to some degree. Doctors are good and seeing one when needed is fine as long as you know what you are doing, spirit man. Do what you must for good health but be aware and alert to your heart. Look at your circumstances and ask, "Who do I believe?" How is the answer related to your situation?

You must always be aware of your dominion and how it works for and applies to you. Don't give away your authority. You can't read the Bible and believe it about good health while you hear a bad report from the doctor and believe him.

As we learn to know ourselves as perfect children of our Spirit Father the power and authority of His realm will infiltrate all our existence flowing outward from the new spirit man if we stay focused on His report and don't become distracted by any report from another source. He wants to tell us who we are and what He has given us as His children. Our conditioning to go to the world for advice and answers must transition to looking within for His answers for us.

You cannot serve two masters, a doctor can help you but how you judge the report is how you will apply your having dominion in your existence. If you are told the condition is a serious threat and you are not attentive to the spirit dimension within, you will authorize the negative report as effective against you. Don't judge your spirit connection based on existing conditions. Walk by faith and not by sight. Out of your heart flow the forces of your life. Reorient those forces to The True report at all times. This transition is going to take persistence on your part.

Note: The purpose of medicine is restoring health. Don't quit taking meds unless the doctor clears you to do so. Gage your maturity and stay focused on Daddy's report until you grow your way out of the situation.

Jesus said allow the "candle" his place and be cautious how you judge the world around you in relation to you, victim or victor. Be cautious whose report you authorize as it relates to you. Stay focused on the perfect son and how you deserve all the good the Lord intends for you in every area; health, finances, relationships.

Here's my experience in this. We are so conditioned to live by the dictates of the mind. It is incapable of this life experience. It must be retrained to serve the recreated man. No amount of biblical information will accomplish the retraining but it can unknowingly set us up for failure by ignoring the spirit.

You must at least read these two books over and over until you gain your insight into the scriptures on your own. Try to find other people who have the same enlightenment within the community of the kingdom and spend time with them.

Don't fall for the world's counterfeits.

You must establish new thinking habits of yourself as spirit, as His child, and then consider meditation, as described earlier, which is a rearrangement of life and a new order of how you function daily. Quiet times of thought and reading will give the Teacher an opportunity to guide you into all Truth. The Lord works with thoughts, sometimes He will initiate them and other times He will lead them but you must be alert.

Enjoy the Lord and allow Him to have enjoyment in you. df

ABOUT THE AUTHOR

Dusty Farrell is a lifelong Christian and a Bible teacher. He lives in central Texas, has been married thirty-five years and is a grandfather. He is a successful business man since the age of sixteen, forty years.

www.dustyfarrell.com

www.ingramcontent.com/pod-product-compliance
Lightning Source LLC
Chambersburg PA
CBHW071840020426
42331CB00007B/1798